This is Ron.

Ron got a dog.
This is Ron's dog.

Ron and his dog trot off to the pond.

Ron spots a frog
at the pond.

It is hot at the pond.

Ron is hot and the dog is hot.

The dog trots into the pond.
The dog is not hot.

Ron hops on the spot.
Ron is hot but he is not
fond of the pond.

Then Ron spots a log.
The log is next to the pond.
He hops onto the log.

The frog hops onto the log.

Ron sits on top of the log.
He dips his legs in the pond.
Ron is not hot and Ron's
dog is not hot.

The frog is fond of the pond.
Ron's dog is fond of the pond.
Ron is fond of the pond as well.